Bird on the Wing
&
Overnight Mountain Snow

Haiku & Senryu

Judith E.P. Johnson

Also by Judith E.P. Johnson

Mountain Moods (VDL Publications, 1997)
Gatherers (VDL Publications, 1998)
Fragments (VDL Publications, 2000)
Selected Poems (CD, 7 RPH, 2001)
Snapshot (Regal Press, 2003)
Landmarks (Ginninderra Press, 2005)
Alone at the Window (Ginninderra Press, 2012)
Between Two Moons (Ginninderra Press, 2015)
Waking from Dreams (Ginninderra Press, 2016)
Where it Leads (Ginninderra Press, 2018)
Only the Waves (Ginninderra Press, 2019)
Briefly in Spring (Ginninderra Press, 2020)
Day Moon Fading (Ginninderra Press, 2021)
Earth from the Moon (Ginninderra Press, 2022)
A Christmas Posy (Ginninderra Press, 2023)
Holding the Moment (with Debra Johnson Fast, Forty South, 2025)

Acknowledgements

The author has had many haiku published in journals, online, and presented on radio. The haiku in *Bird on the Wing & Overnight Mountain Snow* are all new except for those which have appeared in *Kô*, *Echidna Tracks*, and *Under the Same Moon: Fourth Australian Haiku Anthology*, edited by Lyn Reeves, Vanessa Proctor, and Rob Scott.

Special thanks are due to Peter Macrow, my children Karen, Debra and Craig, Jane Williams for editing this book, and Katherine Johnson for the cover design.

Bird on the Wing &
Overnight Mountain Snow
Copyright©2026 Judith E P Johnson
ISBN: 978-1-76109-718-8
First published 2026 by
GINNINDERRA PRESS
PO Box 2 Bentleigh 3042
ginninderrapress.com.au

For Graeme

Preface

Wherever I am, whatever I am doing, there is always the possibility of a haiku moment. When I first started writing haiku I was inspired by a friend, the poet Peter Macrow, who said, 'The impact of the haiku moment is achieved in part by surprise in overlooked beauty.' I also returned again and again to Lee Gurga's idea in *Haiku: A Poet's Guide* of 'the importance of internal connections.' These ideas, along with certain formal conceptions, are at the heart of the practice of haiku. Haiku is not just writing but a way of experiencing.

Haiku offers us a small structure with which to think. In a sudden vision, haiku reveal hidden or secret meanings, within the realities of everyday life. Sometimes these realities are in the things themselves, objects we know or experiences we have, at other times they are in the language we use. The best haiku are those that take one's own experience as their material. When one begins to think with haiku surprises begin to appear everywhere, and daily life takes on a new richness, in turns enlightening and enchanting. Haiku has a certain power to take one's breath away.

This book, *Bird on the Wing & Overnight Mountain Snow*, is a double volume that combines haiku and senryu, as with all my books since *Alone at the Window* in 2012. Haiku observes nature in all seasons. Senryu covers all aspects of human nature or culture. Haiku and senryu are often combined in one poem. Originating in Japan the three-line 5-7-5 syllable count has changed to accommodate differences in the English language. In

The Art of Haiku, Stephen Addis asserts, 'English is more compact than Japanese,' often resulting in works fewer than seventeen syllables. We also need not stick to three lines, two or even one will do. However, there is a risk that the reader might not recognise it as haiku.

When the haiku moment occurs the difficulty is to put it into words but occasionally a haiku appears complete. Often, part of the process is wording and rewording until the observation is obvious. Haiku aims at poetic revelation but is equally a form of elementary observation, a portable thought, a way of seeing, and of locating awe, wonder, humility, and humour. Haiku has no preamble, no explanation, no detailed description, allowing the image to form in one's mind. It is a short and concise form that at its most effective delivers a satisfying haiku moment – 'oh!' The world is revealed. The wonder is released.

Judith E.P. Johnson

Bird on the Wing

daybreak
walking with me
my shadow

I am here
a bird calls
in forest silence

bird on the wing
into the sky
I fly with you

moonshine
in lawn grasses
morning mushrooms

distant snow
fog on my breath
frost under foot

praising spring blooms
don't forget
the winter jasmine

nursery
waiting for adoption
the potted plants

sun-kissed
spring bulbs
from the underworld

but for snow
the swirling wind
invisible

sunny windowsill
lawn daisies
in a saucer

down the hill
from each house
a different view

sunlit and high
in forest leaves
bits of sky

mountain view
breathtaking
the steep climb

how small
the pot-bound lavender
in the ground

your letter
in my hand
keeping in touch

parsley
its green taste
garden fresh

lizard's water dish
a snake
comes too

leafy birdsong
after clearfelling
only the sun

new resort
before tourism
the smell of blood

bushy suburb
little kerbside crosses
for roadkill

silent garden
where is it the bird
that calls and calls?

onion weeds
at the bottom of the garden
fairy bells

first born
like no other
the new parents

tourist
a flock of sparrows
into the elms

albatross wingspan
poised in flight
labelled

toddler
grandma's beads
reaching her ankles

footbridge
in creek sunlight
little fishes

snow it's snowing
in garden silence
children's laughter

rarefied air
I walk through
sacred forest

wayside bud
dried in my pocket
perfumes my fingers

snow-spotted sky
snow-spotted path
the grey dawn

icy wind
taking my breath away
snow-covered mountain

deserted house
empty windows shine
with moonlight

rivulet track
all over me
the mountain mist

rising
a flock of seagulls
my feet in the sand

looking in a birdcage
what's it like
looking out?

low tide
a seagull's footprints
rise into flight

street manhole
a skink
looks around

between buildings
appearing and disappearing
the Harbour Bridge

slipping my grasp
the tail-end
of a dream

walking through leaves
the whisper
of time passing

old photo
you, me, the children
all young

for a moment
this gift we share
time

plane leaf falling
caught mid-air
pressed between poems

camping
child hands clapping
mosquitos

too long this life
not to fall
in love with spring

heads bowed
a row of sunflowers
shed their seeds

Devonshire tea
women
watching other women

bobbing
in the birdbath
half-eaten apple

birds and bees
my thoughts too
have wings

strutting
amongst displaying peacocks
a rooster crows

howling winds
park leaves
leap from the path

sun showers
weed-tangled lawn
flowering

breeze passing
through park roses
thoughts of home

sunlight
through a stained-glass window
the coloured altar cloth

mountain snow melting
in the sun
white blossoms appear

leaves flying
shadows of summer
blown away

jewel box
great grandmother's
precious stories

still there
yesterday's beach
a shell in my hand

you look like my mother
a stranger
shouts us our lunch

gulls cry
a sea urchin
at the water's edge

autumn ripe
ready to drop
the golden quince

rain passing
the warmth
of damp sunshine

rose full blown
collapses
into my hand

floating leaves
filling the room
dream's afterimage

my own company
better
than none at all

out of nothing
my life into nothing
what is nothing?

tiny rainbows
for a moment
party bubbles

reaching
into memory
I find you in the spring

in full bloom
altogether
the park flowers

climbing rose
what makes you reach out
to hold another?

reading
someone else's life
fills my time

indoors fussing around
outdoors
the sun setting

as stones go
I seem to have gathered
a lot of moss

suburban fence
a goshawk eyes
the rabbit hutch

fresh bud in a vase
opens
when I'm not looking

sea spray
drifting across the beach
dotterels

dreamy salt air
a sudden wave
catches me

snow melting
around fruit trees
the daffodils

at last
spring leaves
soften the trimmed hedge

meeting
at the crossroads
a parting of the ways

old shed
jasmine flowers
at the broken window

dark cupboard
doors closed
on a life we shared

flutter of wings
a sparrow circles
the kitchen

drifting park leaves
the path and lawn
as one

spring growth
hum of bees
on the honeyed air

long hair windblown
a glimpse
of butterfly earrings

today
I pick plums ripening
yesterday

birds, cats, stars
dogs and daisies
grandma's button box

winged insect
caught in flight
amber pendant

throwing out
an old diary
I keep its secrets

plum blossoms
filling the sky
between plum blossoms

looping
along the handrail
tiny caterpillars

roadside verge
covering a barbed-wire fence
briar roses

old country road
glimpse
of a headstone

river reeds
now you see it, now you don't
little brown frog

out of park trees
the wind passes me
in a flurry of leaves

picking up a stone tool
I give it back
to the midden

luminous
in ancient gloom
orange fungi

little steps
the toddler
holding my finger

going home
I meet you starting out
late sunshine

spring garden
mother and toddler
share forget-me-nots

reading
I return from afar
the morning gone

cool winds
a cobweb
in the nesting box

gusty treetops
a shower
of bark and gumnuts

sudden wing beat
in forest darkness
a bush moth

rippling waves
of an inland sea
desert sand

warm sea breeze
somewhere
a guitarist singing

holiday
still with me
sand in my shoes

playing in park leaves
an old man
and his dog

whence comes the wind
soft with leaves
and love songs

self portrait
the person
you tell me you are

respite
getting away
from herself

hearing what you say
I listen
to what you mean

keeping me awake
the problem
I'm sleeping on

sunlit leaf shadows
my thoughts
and fairy wrens

old days, old ways
in her cabinet
collectables

stranded high and dry
a nautilus shell
on my shelf

my image
in great grandmother's mirror
her image

lemon tree drip line
a circle
of skeleton leaves

super moon
the night
bright as day

bright lights
moving over the city
space station

promenade band
beating time
the incoming tide

following me
round the old house
a cold draught

barefoot
in the dark hallway
a cricket grabs my toe

one porch light
shining
suburban darkness

poem read
he surfaces
from the memory

missionary road
foreshore middens
left behind

memorial bench
we sit
where the old couple dreamed

camphor wood chest
closed so long
memories overflow

long life
in a few words
her story

steady rain
scattered ashes
settle into the earth

everywhere
blending into darkness
scented flowers

beneath this plaque
nothing
disturbs your ashes

turning from the sun
earth's dark side
in moonlight

maintenance
so much body
to carry my thoughts

days running away
all these years
into my body

curled in a chair
my book and I
not there

darkness comes
with sleep
stars appear

houses silent
darkness fills the rooms
with light

too many lives
to relive
grandma's bookshelf

walking home
a kiss in the dark
so long ago

out of nowhere
into nowhere
a shooting star

earth turning
in darkness
hold me

Overnight Mountain Snow

mountain ledge
the depth
of valley silence

widow
her husband's voice
in her voice

cool breeze
through she-oaks
the smell of hot sand

summer sun
counting apples
on the new tree

kind words
read and reread
into memory

honeyed fingerprint
out of nowhere
dot ant

touching an old toy
the feel
of childhood

deep sea sky
whales and schools of fish
flying

antique table
longstanding
clawed footprints

sunrise walk
behind the mountain
full moon setting

time and tide
all round the old house
life's debris

gone
in my neck of the woods
all the trees

only the ant knows
how heavy
the grain of sugar

alone
the silence of your words
repeating

warm kitchen
from the cupboard
a cold draught

heading
on an old letter
Burn This

coming in
the front door
her world

city park
larger than life
statues of mortals

cloud lifting
overnight
mountain snow

cup of tea
she pours memories
into my memory

lullaby
soothing the baby
and mother

grey rain
in bush debris
little sun orchid

behind each haiku
a long story
untold

her mind elsewhere
sunlit butterfly
unnoticed

elderly neighbour
each night
walks the four corners

sheen of sky and sea
in a glass case
shell necklaces

stars beyond starlight this sand underfoot

earth turning
always
I am the right way up

leaving the lift
she holds the door
with her stick

pink camellia
out on a limb
the red flower

bush track
taking me
where someone else has been

beneath
the bubbling brook
rock shadows

sunrise river
distant mountain
pink with snow

dry eyed
I hear the tears
in her voice

high wind howling
along the shore
silent middens

morning view
opening the blind
my small world

palette of summer
in a bowl
fresh fruit salad

overcast day
sound of the bread knife
cutting seeds

sunshine
after rain the hum
of lawnmowers

leaving city chaos
the peace
of wild places

dark forest
going deeper
into myself

empty shadows
under the house
lattice sunshine

opening a window
I let in
all the flowers of spring

sunlit treetops
above morning shadows
birds preening

playgroup
seen and not heard
the mothers

night long
no one hears
the moon passing

mountain road
a glimpse of wattles
holding the sun

lightning strike
a young tree
changes shape

plasticine
in father's big hands
tiny dinosaurs

shopping, cooking
for a moment
food on the table

words on the page
even these
the wind blows away

waiting for tomorrow
suddenly
the day after

for grandma
a cup of tea
from the toy teapot

not your smile
most important now
the mask you wear

shop window reflections
a man stops
to look again

drifting
at the workshop doorway
snowdrops

morning light
across the hills
floods the river

the bright room
she inhabits alone
in darkness

pink feather
deserted
the old aviary

gumnuts and shells
I walk the edge
of land and sea

souvenir shop
an oyster shell
holds the fishing village

travelling
all the way home
your postcard

everything
in its place
the falling leaves

ragdoll
mother's needle and thread
make her smile

pastel colours
on the night air
sweet peas

birthday cake
a whiff
of long ago candles

rivulet track
rising into trees
the morning mist

pleasantries
sometimes in sunshine
I glimpse your shadows

snow-cloud gloom
nowhere
the sun-loving skink

underground
mighty the earth-moving worm
to the ant

weathered tree stump
protruding from the sand
dragon head

sleeping child
father draws the curtains
full moon

Brahms' lullaby
this forgotten song
keeps me awake

following the road
away from home
takes me back

little green frog
on my microwave
a magnet

returning
after a long absence
the bush

calm waters
time
for reflection

bright sun
filling the house
with shadows

thoughts
interrupting my thoughts
another thought

once other rooms
this room
now a museum

digging into the past
she finds
another bone to chew

one day
I shall throw these old things out
but not today

morning mist
clearing
the sunlit mountain

dressing-up box
the musty glitter
of old clothes

as words flow
into story
the minutes

warm breeze
housebound snail
a butterfly out of sight

washed up
in a bottle
message from the future

leaf shadows
this bush track
leading me astray

dawn stillness
from a stone cottage
a plume of blue smoke

where the old ones walked
I walk
footprints lost in sand

leaving
I watch you disappear
into your life

fragile shell
tossed in breakers
intact

grandma's shelf
each ornament
a family story

colours changing
in muted sunshine
the first leaf falls

describing
each person tells
a different story

Saturday night
somewhere
a band tuning up

gone so long
in family laughter
your voice

frozen
the dark earth holds
blossoms of spring

watching the ant
I wonder
who's watching me

remote beach
a rowing boat sinks deeper
into sand

crowded room
empty
without you

since you were here
fast flowing the river
under the bridge

careful with wishes
granted
everything changes

beyond the mountain
somewhere
a valley mist of dreams

The author. Photo by Debra Johnson Fast

www.ingramcontent.com/pod-product-compliance
Lightning Source LLC
Chambersburg PA
CBHW071852070526
44583CB00016B/1650